W9-BWF-448

It's About Time!™

...All About the Seasons

Joanne Randolph

PowerKiDS
press™
New York

Published in 2008 by The Rosen Publishing Group, Inc.
29 East 21st Street, New York, NY 10010

First Edition

Book Design: Kate Laczynski
Photo Researcher: Nicole Pristash

Photo Credits: All photos © Shutterstock.com.

Library of Congress Cataloging-in-Publication Data

Randolph, Joanne.
 All about the seasons / Joanne Randolph. — 1st ed.
     p. cm. — (It's about time!)
 Includes bibliographical references and index.
 ISBN-13: 978-1-4042-3768-1 (lib. bdg.)
 ISBN-10: 1-4042-3768-2 (lib. bdg.)
 1. Seasons—Juvenile literature. I. Title.
 QB637.4.R36 2008
 508.2—dc22
                                                    2006037189

Manufactured in the United States of America

Contents

We have winter, spring, summer, and fall.

These are the four seasons. We'll learn about them all.

The first season brings us
ice and snow.

From December to March,
cold winds blow.

This cold season is winter.
It sure can be lots of fun.

With skating and snowmen,
who needs the Sun?

From March to June,
the next season takes hold.

Lots of rain and warmer air
push out the cold.

Spring is the name of this time of year.

Flowers grow, children play, and warm weather is here.

From June through September, sunshine is king.

Hot days and hot nights are what the next season brings.

When we think of the summer, we think of the heat.

We think of cold **lemonade** and running on the beach in bare feet.

From September to December, the last season stays.

The air cools, **leaves** turn colors, and we have shorter days.

This time of year is called autumn or fall.

We **carve** pumpkins, **rake** leaves, and play some football.

Each season brings its own special fun.

Which season do you like best? Can you pick just one?

Words to Know

carve

leaves

lemonade

rake

Index

Web Sites

Due to the changing nature of Internet links, PowerKids Press has developed an online list of Web sites related to the subject of this book. This site is updated regularly. Please use this link to access the list: www.powerkidslinks.com/iat/seasons/